STATE REPORTS

Western
Great Lakes

ILLINOIS ★ IOWA ★ MINNESOTA ★ WISCONSIN

By
Thomas G. Aylesworth
Virginia L. Aylesworth

CHELSEA HOUSE PUBLISHERS
New York   Philadelphia

Produced by James Charlton Associates
New York, New York.

First Printing

1   3   5   7   9   8   6   4   2

Library of Congress Cataloging-in-Publication Data

Aylesworth, Thomas G.
    Western Great Lakes: Illinois, Iowa, Minnesota, Wisconsin/by
Thomas G. Aylesworth, Virginia L. Aylesworth.
    p. cm. — (State reports)
    Includes bibliographical references and index.
    Summary: Discusses the geographical, historical, and cultural aspects of Illinois, Iowa,
Minnesota, and Wisconsin.
    ISBN 0-7910-1046-5
        0-7910-1393-6 (pbk.)
    1. Lake States—Juvenile literature. 2. Illinois—Juvenile literature. 3. Iowa—Juvenile literature.
4. Minnesota—Juvenile literature. 5. Wisconsin—Juvenile literature. [1. Lake States. 2. Illinois.
3. Iowa. 4. Minnesota. 5. Wisconsin.] I. Aylesworth, Virginia L. II. Title. III. Series: Aylesworth,
Thomas G. State reports.
J F551.A955 1991
977—dc20
                                90-28834
                                CIP
                                AC

Contents

Wisconsin

Illinois

The state seal of Illinois, designed by the secretary of state Sharon Tyndale, was first used in 1868. The current seal is the third in Illinois history. In the center of the circular seal is an American eagle holding a shield with stars and stripes representing the 13 original states. In the eagle's beak is a scroll bearing the state motto. Under the shield is an olive branch, symbolizing peace, and nearby is a boulder with two dates, 1818 (the year Illinois entered the Union) and 1868 (the year the seal was adopted). Around the top of the circle is inscribed, "Seal of the State of Illinois," and at the bottom is the date August 26th, 1818—the date the first state constitution was adopted.

State Flag

The Illinois state flag, adopted in 1915, bears a modification of the state seal set on a white background.

State Motto

State Sovereignty, National Union

Inscribed on the state seal, first adopted in 1818, this motto reflects the idea that the state rules itself, but is subservient to the nation.

Canoeing on Devils Kitchen Lake.

WISCONSIN

IOWA

INDIANA

MISSOURI

KENTUCKY

ILLINOIS

■ GALENA
● Freeport
● **Rockford**
● Oregon
● De Kalb
● Elgin
● Wheaton
● **Chicago**
LISLE ■ BROOKFIELD
● Aurora
● Joliet
● Waukegan

● East Moline
● Rock Island

● Kankakee

● Galesburg

● **Peoria**
● Pekin
● Normal
● Bloomington
■ NAUVOO RESTORATION
● Rantoul
● Champaign
● Danville
● Urbana

● Quincy
■ Petersburg
★ Springfield
● Decatur
■ Charleston
● Jacksonville
■ LINCOLN HOME NATIONAL HISTORICAL SITE

Mississippi River

● Alton

● Granite City
● Belleville

Wabash River

Ohio River

N
△

★ State Capital
● Cities or towns
■ OF SPECIAL INTEREST

0 10 20   40   60   80   100   120   Miles
0 10 20 40 60 80 100 120 140 160 180 200 Kilometres

The state capitol building in Springfield.

State Capital

The first capital was at Kaskaskia (1818-20). It was then moved to Vandalia (1820-39), and finally, in 1839, to Springfield. The capitol building was completed in 1888 at a cost of $4.5 million. It is designed in the form of a Latin cross and is in both the classical Greek and classical Roman styles. The dome rises to a height of 361 feet, and the outer walls are built of limestone.

State Name and Nicknames

Illinois was named by the French explorer, Robert Cavelier, Sieur de La Salle, in 1679. It was the French spelling of the Indian word, *illini*, which means warrior or member of the Illinois tribe.

The most common nickname for Illinois is the *Prairie State* because of the vast prairies in the territory. It is also called the *Corn State* because of the importance of that crop to the farmers of the region. Illinois has an official state slogan, adopted in 1955—"The Land of Lincoln"—since it was here that the Great Emancipator began his political career.

State Flower

In 1907, Illinois schoolchildren voted for the state flower from a list of three blooms—the violet, the wild rose, and the goldenrod. The violet, *Viola pedatifida*, won and it was decreed the state flower in 1908.

The violet is the state flower.

State Tree

The children also voted in 1907 for a state tree, and the native oak was selected in 1908. But there are two oak trees native to the state, the northern red oak and the white oak, so the children voted a second time. The white oak, *Quercus alba*, was adopted in 1973.

State Bird

Schoolchildren also chose the cardinal, *Cardinalis cardinalis*, as state bird in 1929.

State Animal

The white-tailed deer, *Odocoileus virginianus*, was named the state animal in 1982.

State Insect

The monarch butterfly, *Danaus plexippus*, was adopted as state insect in 1975.

State Language

English has been the state language of Illinois since 1969.

State Mineral

Fluorite was named state mineral in 1965.

State Song

In 1925, "Illinois," words by Charles H. Chamberlain and music by Archibald Johnston, was made the state song.

Population

The population of Illinois in 1990 was 11,466,682, making

The cardinal is the state bird.

it the sixth most populous state. There are 203.5 persons per square mile—83.3 percent of the population live in towns and cities. About 93 percent of the people in Illinois were born in the United States. The largest groups of foreign-born came from Mexico and Poland. Other groups include Germans, Greeks, Indians, Italians, Russians, British, and Yugoslavians.

Geography

Bounded on the north by Wisconsin, on the east by Lake Michigan, Indiana, and Kentucky, on the south by Kentucky and Missouri, and on the west by Missouri and Iowa, Illinois has an area of 56,345 square miles, making it the 24th largest state. The climate is temperate, with cold winters and hot summers.

The highest point in the state, at 1,235 feet, is Charles Mound, in Jo Daviess County. The lowest, at 279 feet, is in Alexander County on the Mississippi River. There are prairies and fertile plains throughout the state, and hills in the south. The major waterways of the state are the Mississippi, Chicago, Des Plaines, Illinois, Sangamon, Spoon, Rock, Fox, Wabash, and Ohio rivers. The largest lake in the state is Carlyle Lake.

Industries

The principal industries of Illinois are trade, finance, insurance, foods, and agriculture. The chief manufactured products are machinery, electric and electronic equipment, metals, chemicals, printing, and publishing.

Agriculture

The chief crops of the state are corn, soybeans, wheat, oats, and hay. Illinois is also a livestock state, and there are estimated to be some 1.9 million cattle, 5.6 million hogs and pigs, 140,000 sheep, and 3.76 million chickens and turkeys on its farms. Oak, hickory, maple, and cottonwood trees are harvested. Crushed stone, cement, sand, and gravel are important mineral resources. Commercial fishing brings in some $304,000 a year.

Government

The governor of Illinois is elected to a four-year term, as are the lieutenant governor, attorney general, secretary of state, comptroller, and treasurer. The state legislature, called the general assembly, which meets annually, consists of a senate of 59 members and a house of

An afternoon of sailing on Lake Michigan, which borders Illinois.

representatives of 118 members. The senators are elected to four-year terms and the representatives to two-year terms. The most recent state constitution was adopted in 1970. In addition to its two U.S. senators, Illinois has 20 representatives in the U.S. House of Representatives. The state has 22 votes in the electoral college.

History

Before the Europeans arrived, what was to become Illinois was populated by prehistoric Indians known as Mound Builders. They were supplanted by "The Illinois Confederacy," a group of tribes that included the Cahokia, the Kaskaskia, the Michigamea, the Moingwena, the Peoria, and the Tamaroa. However, these Illinois Indians, who belonged to the Algonkian family, were almost wiped out by attacking Iroquois in 1680. Other Indian tribes of the time were the Chippewa, the Ottawa, the Potawatomi, the Sauk (or Sac), the Fox, the Winnebago, the Kickapoo, the Mascouten, the Piankashaw, and the Shawnee.

Father Jacques Marquette and Louis Jolliet were the first to explore the territory along the Mississippi, in 1673. Later they explored the Illinois River, and Marquette founded a mission at a Kaskaskia Indian village (near present-day Utica) in 1675. In 1699, other French priests founded a mission at Cahokia, which was the first permanent town in Illinois. Kaskaskia was founded by priests in 1703, and in 1717, Illinois became a part of the French colony of Louisiana. After losing the French and Indian War, the French gave the region to England in 1763.

During the Revolutionary War, George Rogers Clark captured Kaskaskia and Cahokia from the British in 1778, and Illinois became a part of Virginia.

Virginia turned the territory over to the federal government in 1784, and Illinois became part of the Northwest Territory in 1787. In 1800, it became part of the Indiana Territory, and in 1809, Congress created the Illinois Territory. In 1818, Illinois became the 21st state in the Union.

In 1825, the Erie Canal opened the midwest by linking the Great Lakes with the eastern states. Illinois boomed. Canals were dug and railroads were built. Most of the people of Illinois favored the Union during the Civil War, and about 255,000 served in the Union Army.

After the war, industry increased and Chicago became the center of grain and meat-packing in the country. In 1893, Chicago had its first World's Fair—the Columbian Exposition.

During World War I, thousands of troops were trained at Great Lakes Naval Training Center and Fort Sheridan. Like most other states, Illinois suffered in the Great Depression of the 1930s. The return to prosperity began with the discovery of oil in the southeast.

During World War II, more than 800 aircraft and aircraft-parts plants, plus many other defense factories, turned out equipment and war materials. The northern part of the state became the largest steel-producing region in the country, and the Argonne National Laboratory became the leading research center.

During the Korean War, more than half the Illinois National Guard was sent to active service. Today, Illinois is a giant in agriculture, industry, and transportation.

Sports

Illinois is a sport-conscious state and always has been. In 1896 in Chicago, the University of Chicago beat the University of Iowa in the first basketball game using five men on each side. In 1901 the first American Bowling Congress National Championship Tournament was held in Chicago. On the

A beautiful afternoon for baseball at Wrigley Field, home of the Chicago Cubs.

collegiate level, the NCAA national basketball championship was won by Loyola University of Chicago in 1963, and the National Invitation Tournament, by Bradley University (1957, 1960, 1964, 1982), De Paul University (1945), and Southern Illinois University (1967). In football, the Rose Bowl has been won by the University of Illinois (1947, 1952, 1964) and Northwestern University (1949).

On the professional level, Chicago is home to several teams. The Cubs of the National League play baseball at Wrigley Field, and the White Sox of the American League play in Comiskey Park. The Bears of the National Football League hold their games in Soldier Field, and the Bulls of the National Basketball Association and Blackhawks of the National Hockey League share Chicago Stadium.

Major Cities

Chicago (population 3,005,072). Settled in 1803, the territory was mapped in 1673 by Louis Jolliet, and the first trading post was established in 1796. The city didn't start its real growth as an industrial and cultural center until the mid-1800s. The name came from the Indian word *Checagou*, which seems to have several meanings. Chicago is a city of beautiful parks, monumental architecture, and dynamic people.

Things to see in Chicago: Chicago Public Library Cultural Center, Monadnock Building (1889-93), Rookery (1886), Chicago Board of Trade (1929), Sears Tower, Chicago Mercantile Exchange, Navy Pier, John Hancock Center, Water Tower (1969), Chicago *Tribune* Tower, Wrigley Building, Newberry Library (1887), Robie House, Jane Addams' Hull House (1856), Art Institute of Chicago, Museum of Contemporary Art, Terra Museum of American Art, Peace Museum, Chicago Historical

A prehistoric creature is displayed at the Field Museum of Natural History, in the Grant Park area of Chicago.

Society, Chicago Academy of Sciences, Adler Planetarium, John G. Shedd Aquarium, Field Museum of Natural History, Chicago Fire Academy, Museum of Science and Industry, Oriental Institute Museum, Morton B. Weiss Museum of Judaica, Du Sable Museum of African-American History, Chicago Temple, Moody Church, Our

Lady of Sorrows Basilica, Lincoln Park Zoological Gardens, Lincoln Park Conservatory, and the Garfield Park Conservatory.

Rockford (population 139,712). Founded in 1834, the second-largest city in the state is located on the Rock River. The first settlers were from New England, but today much of the population is of Swedish and Italian descent. Rockford is an important industrial city.

Things to see in Rockford: Tinker Swiss Cottage (1865), Time Museum, Midway Village/Rockford Museum Center, Burpee Museum of Natural History, Rockford Art Museum, Zitelman Scout Museum, John Erlander Home (1871), Sinnissippi Park, Rockford Trolley, and *Forest City Queen.*

Springfield (population 100,054). Settled in 1819, the capital city of Illinois was laid out near the geographical center of the state. The city is most famous as the home of Abraham Lincoln for the 25 years before he was elected president.

Things to see in Springfield:
State Capitol, Illinois State Museum, Old State Capitol State Historic Site, Lincoln's Tomb State Historic Site, Lincoln Home National Historic Site, Oliver P. Parks Telephone Museum, Dana-Thomas House State Historic Site (1902-04), Lincoln Depot, Lincoln-Herndon Building, Vachel Lindsay Home (1846), Thomas Rees Memorial Carillon, Lincoln Memorial Garden and Nature Center, Executive Mansion, Edwards Place (1833), and Henson Robinson Zoo.

Abraham Lincoln's Springfield home of sixteen years is now the Lincoln Home National Historic Site. Three of his sons were born there.

Places to Visit

The National Park Service maintains two areas in the state of Illinois: Lincoln Home National Historic Site and Shawnee National Forest. In addition, there are 73 state recreation areas.

Antioch: Hiram Butrick Sawmill. This is a working replica of an 1839 waterpowered sawmill that was the center of the town.

Brookfield: Brookfield Zoo. One of the world's finest zoos features indoor rain forests and dolphin shows.

Cahokia: Cahokia Courthouse State Historic Site. A restoration of the oldest house in the state, which was built around 1737.

Charleston: Lincoln Log Cabin State Historic Site. The Thomas Lincoln Log Cabin, where the family lived after 1837, has been reconstructed here.

East St. Louis: Katherine Dunham Museum. A collection of African and Caribbean artifacts collected by the dancer and choreographer is exhibited.

Elgin: Fox River Trolley Museum. Early trolleys and railway equipment can be seen and rides can be taken on early 1900s cars.

Galena: Ulysses S. Grant Home State Historic Site. This house was given to Grant by his native city after the Civil War.

Galesburg: Carl Sandburg State Historical Site. Built in 1874, this was the home of the famous poet and historian.

Glenview: Hartung's Automotive Museum. More than 100 antique autos and trucks are displayed here.

Havana: Dickson Mounds State Museum. Remains of prehistoric Indian life can be seen here.

Highwood: Fort Sheridan. The fort was founded in 1887 and contains 94 old buildings and exhibits of military history.

La Grange: Historic District. Buildings dating from the late nineteenth and early twentieth centuries, including some designed by Frank Lloyd Wright, can be seen.

Lisle: Morton Aboretum. This bucolic area of about 1,500 acres contains some 5,000 kinds of trees and other plants.

Macomb: Clarence Watson/Wiley Schoolhouse Museum. This restored 1877 one-room schoolhouse still contains many of the original fixtures.

Naperville: Naper Settlement. This 12-acre outdoor history museum with 25 buildings recreates a northern Illinois town of the nineteenth century.

Nauvoo: Nauvoo Restoration. Nauvoo was founded as a Mormon community. The Brigham Young Home and many other structures here are open to the public.

Oak Brook: Old Graue Mill and Museum. This restored 1852 mill is the only operating waterpowered gristmill in the state.

Oak Park: Frank Lloyd Wright Home and Studio. Several buildings designed by the architect, including his own home and studio, and the Unity Temple, can be seen here.

Oregon: Stronghold Castle. This authentic old English castle was built in the early part of the century.

Petersburg: Lincoln's New Salem State Historic Site. This is a reconstruction of the town of New Salem when Lincoln lived there.

Princeton: Owen Lovejoy Homestead. Built in 1838, this was the home of the abolitionist preacher as well as a stop on the Underground Railroad.

Rock Island: Black Hawk State Historic Site. This is the site of the western-most battle of the Revolutionary War.

Salem: William Jennings Bryan Birthplace/Museum. The restored birthplace of the famous orator was built in 1852.

Union: Illinois Railway Museum. Historic and antique railroad cars, engines, and coaches are displayed on the museum's 56 acres.

Vandalia: Vandalia Statehouse State Historic Site. This was built in 1836, when the town was the state capital.

Woodstock: Woodstock Opera House. This restored "Steamboat Gothic" theater dates back to 1889.

Events

There are many events and organizations that schedule activities of various kinds in the state of Illinois. Here are some of them.

Sports: Chicago to Mackinac Races (Chicago), Mid-America Canoe Race (Elgin), Elgin National Road Race (Elgin), Santa Fe Speedway (Hinsdale), Kankakee River Valley Bicycle Classic (Kankakee), Kankakee River Valley Regatta (Kankakee), Western Open Golf Tournament (Oak Brook), Polo (Oak Brook), Montreal Canoe Weekends (Peru), Grand Prix of Karting (Quincy), Rockford Speedway

(Rockford), LPGA Rail Charity Golf Classic (Springfield).

Arts and Crafts: Sommarmarknad (Bishop Hill), Ewing Arts Festival (Bloomington), Chicago International Art Exposition (Chicago), Gold Coast Art Fair (Chicago), Fountain Square Arts Festival (Evanston), Lakefront Art Fair (Evanston), Gladiolus Festival (Kankakee), Greenwich Village Art Fair (Rockford), Clayville Folk Crafts Festival (Springfield).

Music: Hubbard Street Dance Company (Chicago), Mordine and Company (Chicago), Chicago Opera Theater (Chicago), Lyric Opera of Chicago (Chicago), Chicago Symphony (Chicago), Chicago Civic Orchestra (Chicago), Grant Park Symphony (Chicago), Civic Opera (Chicago), Jazz Festival (Chicago), Band Concerts (Elgin), Rootabaga Jazz Festival (Galesburg), Ravinia Festival (Highland Park), International Carillon Festival (Springfield), Municipal Band Concerts (Springfield), Springfield Muni Opera (Springfield).

Entertainment: Bishop Hill Jordbruksdagarna (Bishop Hill), Harvest Frolic (Charleston), St. Patrick's Day Parade (Chicago), Taste of Chicago (Chicago), Air and Water Show (Chicago), Electric Railroad Fair (Elgin),

Custer's Last Stand (Evanston), Antique Town Rod Run (Galena), Geneva Swedish Festival (Geneva), Pet Parade (La Grange), Old Canal Days (Lockport), Joe Naper Day (Naperville), Steamboat Days (Peoria), Winter Wilderness Weekend (Peru), National Sweet Corn Festival (Peru), Burgoo Festival (Peru), Calftown Strassenfest (Quincy), Winter Carnival (Rockford), Mid-America Horse Festival (St. Charles), Maple Syrup Time (Springfield), Illinois State Fair (Springfield).

Tours: Loop Walking Tour (Chicago), June Open House (Galena), Fall Tour of Homes (Galena), Wildflower Pilgrimage (Peru), Candlelight Tour of New Salem (Petersburg).

Theater: The American Passion Play (Bloomington), Illinois Shakespeare Festival (Bloomington), Arie Crown (Chicago), Body Politic (Chicago), Goodman Theater (Chicago), Second City (Chicago), Stage Coach Theater (De Kalb), Poplar Creek Music Theater (Hoffman Estates), Rialto Square Theatre (Joliet), Bicentennial Park Theater (Joliet), *City of Joseph* (Nauvoo), New American Theater (Rockford), Genesius Guild (Rock Island), Centre East for the Arts (Skokie).

It's maple syrup time in the woods of Lincoln Memorial Garden in Springfield.

Famous People

Many famous people were born in the state of Illinois. Here are a few:

Jane Addams 1860-1935, Cedarville. Co-founder of Hull House

Mary Astor 1906-87, Quincy. Academy Award-winning actress: *The Great Lie, The Maltese Falcon*

John Belushi 1949-1982, Chicago. Television and film actor: *Animal House, Neighbors*

Jack Benny 1894-1974, Chicago. Film, television and radio comedian: *To Be or Not To Be*

Harry Blackmun b. 1908, Nashville. Supreme Court justice

Lou Boudreau b. 1917, Harvey. Hall of Fame baseball player

Ray Bradbury b. 1920,

Waukegan. Novelist: *Fahrenheit 451*

William Jennings Bryan 1860-1925, Salem. Orator and presidential candidate

Edgar Rice Burroughs 1875-1950, Chicago. Novelist: *Tarzan* books

Dick Butkus b. 1942, Chicago. Hall of Fame football player

John Chancellor b. 1927, Chicago. Television newsman

Raymond Chandler 1888-1959, Chicago. Novelist: *Farewell, My Lovely*

Jimmy Connors b. 1952, Belleville. Tennis champion

Miles Davis b. 1926, Alton. Jazz trumpeter

Walt Disney 1901-66, Chicago. Animation producer

John Dos Passos 1896-1970, Chicago. Novelist: *Manhattan Transfer, U.S.A.*

Wyatt Earp 1848-1929, Monmouth. Western law officer

James T. Farrell 1904-79, Chicago. Novelist: *The Young Manhood of Studs Lonigan*

Bobby Fischer b. 1943, Chicago. Champion chess player

Harrison Ford b. 1942, Chicago. Film actor: *Star Wars, Raiders of the Lost Ark*

Bob Fosse 1927-87, Chicago. Stage and film director

Betty Friedan b. 1921, Peoria. Feminist

Arthur Goldberg b. 1908, Chicago. Supreme Court justice

Benny Goodman 1909-86, Chicago. Swing clarinetist

Lorraine Hansberry 1930-65, Chicago. Playwright: *A Raisin in the Sun*

Hugh Hefner b. 1926, Chicago. Magazine publisher

Ernest Hemingway 1899-1961, Oak Park. Nobel Prize-winning novelist: *For Whom the Bell Tolls, The Old Man and the Sea*

Charlton Heston b. 1923, Evanston. Academy

Award-winning actor: *Ben Hur, Soylent Green*

Wild Bill Hickock 1837-1876, Troy Grove. Western marshal

Rock Hudson 1925-1985, Winnetka. Film actor: *Giant, Pillow Talk*

Burl Ives b. 1909, Hunt Township. Academy Award-winning actor: *Cat on a Hot Tin Roof*

James Jones 1921-77, Robinson. Novelist: *From Here to Eternity*

Quincy Jones b. 1933, Chicago. Composer and arranger

Gene Krupa 1909-73, Chicago. Jazz drummer

Vachel Lindsay 1879-1931, Springfield. Poet: *The Congo and Other Poems*

Archibald MacLeish 1892-1982, Glencoe. Pulitzer Prize-winning poet: *Conquistador*

Jimmy McPartland b. 1907, Chicago. Jazz cornetist

George Mikan b. 1924, Joliet. Hall of Fame basketball player

Sherrill Milnes b. 1935, Downers Grove. Operatic baritone

Vincente Minnelli 1910-86, Chicago. Film director

Bob Newhart b. 1929, Oak Park. Television actor and comedian: *The Bob Newhart Show, Newhart*

Ken Norton b. 1945, Jacksonville. Heavyweight boxing champion

William S. Paley 1901-1990, Chicago. Founder of CBS

Richard Pryor b. 1940, Peoria. Stage and film comedian: *Silver Streak, Stir Crazy*

Edward M. Purcell b. 1912, Taylorville. Nobel Prize-winning physicist

Ronald Reagan b. 1911, Tampico. Fortieth President of the United States

Jason Robards, Jr. b. 1922, Chicago. Academy Award-winning actor: *All the President's Men, Julia*

Carl Sandburg 1878-1967, Galesburg. Pulitzer Prize-winning poet and

Wild Bill Hickock was a marshal and hero of the Old West.

historian: *Complete Poems*

E. W. Scripps 1854-1926, Rushville. Founder of United Press

John Paul Stevens b. 1920, Chicago. Supreme Court justice

Peter Ueberroth b. 1937, Chicago. Baseball commissioner

Carl Van Doren 1885-1950, Hope. Pulitzer Prize-winning biographer

Mark Van Doren 1894-1972, Hope. Pulitzer Prize-winning poet

James D. Watson b. 1928, Chicago. Nobel Prize-winning biochemist

P. K. Wrigley 1894-1977, Chicago. Chewing gum executive

Florenz Ziegfeld 1869-1932, Chicago. Broadway producer

Colleges and Universities

There are many colleges and universities in Illinois. Here are the more prominent, with their locations, dates of founding, and enrollments:

Augustana College, Rock Island, 1860, 2,267

Aurora University, Aurora, 1893, 2,045

Bradley University, Peoria, 1897, 5,658

Chicago State University, Chicago, 1869, 6,034

College of St. Francis, Joliet, 1874, 1,804

Concordia College, River Forest, 1864, 1,275

De Paul University, Chicago, 1898, 15,387

Eastern Illinois University, Charleston, 1895, 10,427

Elmhurst College, Elmhurst, 1871, 3,007

Illinois Benedictine College, Lisle, 1887, 2,662

Illinois College, Jacksonville, 1829, 813

Illinois Institute of Technology, Chicago, 1892, 6,300

Illinois State University, Normal, 1857, 23,108

Illinois Wesleyan University, Bloomington, 1850, 1,749

Knox College, Galesburg, 1837, 1,029

Lake Forest College, Lake Forest, 1857, 1,124

Lewis University, Romeoville, 1930, 3,500

Loyola University of Chicago, Chicago, 1870, 14,343

Millikin University, Decatur, 1901, 1,805

Mundelein College, Chicago,

1929, 1,102

National College of Education, Evanston, 1886, 7,436

North Central College, Naperville, 1861, 2,555

Northern Illinois University, De Kalb, 1895, 24,443

Northwestern University, Evanston, 1851, 11,554

Olivet Nazarene College, Kankakee, 1907, 1,875

Quincy College, Quincy, 1860, 1,601

Rockford College, Rockford, 1847, 1,372

Roosevelt University, Chicago, 1945, 6,374

Rosary College, River Forest, 1848, 1,767

Rush University, Chicago, 1969, 1,112

Saint Xavier College, Chicago, 1846, 2,653

Southern Illinois University at Carbondale, Carbondale, 1874, 24,596; *at Edwardsville,* Edwardsville, 1971, 11,320

University of Chicago, Chicago, 1891, 9,300

University of Illinois at Chicago, Chicago, 1965, 24,195; *at Urbana-Champaign,* Urbana, 1867, 35,032

Western Illinois University, Macomb, 1899, 12,500

Wheaton College, Wheaton, 1860, 2,548

Where To Get More Information
Illinois Tourist Information Center
310 South Michigan Avenue
Chicago, IL 60604

Iowa

    The state seal of Iowa, adopted in 1847, is circular. In the center is a prairie scene: A pioneer citizen-soldier stands before a plow. In his right hand is an American flag with a liberty cap on top; in his left hand is a rifle. On the ground is a sheaf and a field of standing wheat, and a lead furnace and a pile of pig lead. In the distance is the Mississippi River, on which the steamer *Iowa* is sailing. An eagle flies above the scene with a banner in its beak. On the banner is the state motto. Around the seal is printed "The Great Seal of the State of Iowa."

State Flag

Designed by Mrs. Dixie Cornell Gebhardt and adopted in 1921, the state flag of Iowa consists of three broad vertical stripes of blue, white, and red. In the center of the white stripe is the eagle and banner from the state seal with the word "Iowa" printed below it.

State Motto

Our Liberties We Prize, and Our Rights We Will Maintain

Adopted in 1846, the motto expresses the feelings of the people of the state as they entered the Union.

Hot-air ballooning is a popular sport in Iowa, where the view from above is endless.

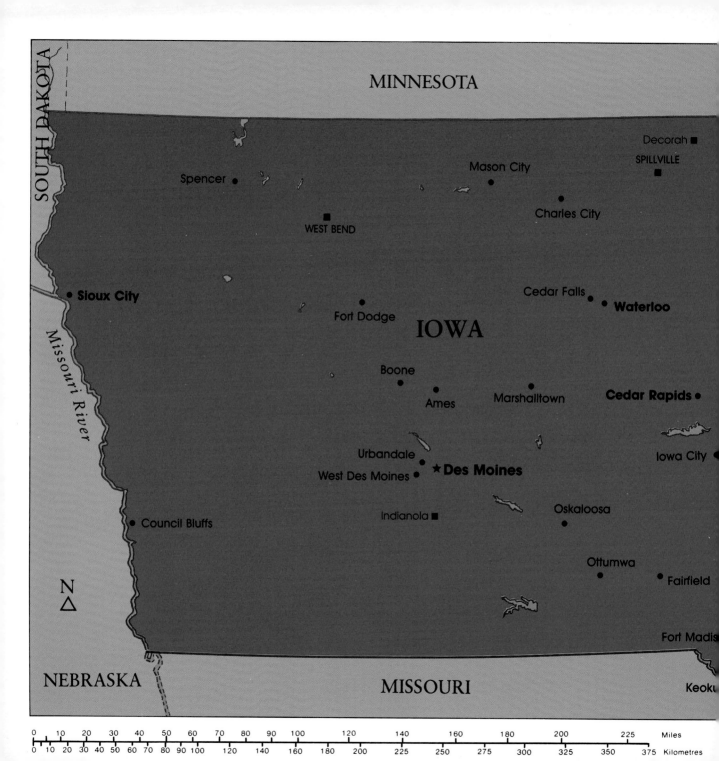

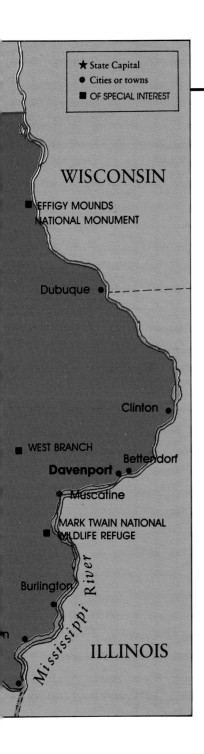

★ State Capital
● Cities or towns
■ OF SPECIAL INTEREST

WISCONSIN

■ EFFIGY MOUNDS
NATIONAL MONUMENT

Dubuque ●

Clinton ●

■ WEST BRANCH

Bettendorf
Davenport ●●

● Muscatine

■ MARK TWAIN NATIONAL
WILDLIFE REFUGE

Burlington ●

Mississippi River

ILLINOIS

State Capital

The first capital of Iowa was Burlington (1838-41). Iowa City became the capital in 1841, and Des Moines in 1857. The capitol building in Des Moines was first occupied in 1884. It has a steel and stone dome covered with gold leaf, and was constructed of Iowa stone, Iowa granite, Missouri limestone, and anamosa from Iowa, Ohio, Minnesota, and Illinois. The original cost of the building was $2,873,294.

The state capitol building in Des Moines.

State Name and Nickname

The Iowa River was named for the Iowa Indians who lived in the area, and the state was named after the river. The Indian word was *Ayuxwa*, which meant "one who puts to sleep." It was spelled by French explorers as "Ayoua" and by the English as "Ioway."

Although it is unofficial, the nickname for the state is the *Hawkeye State*, a tribute to the Indian chief Black Hawk.

State Flower

In 1897, the wild rose, *Rosa pratincola*, was named the state flower of Iowa.

State Tree

The white oak, *Quercus alba*, was designated the state tree in 1961.

State Bird

The eastern goldfinch, *Spinus tristis*, was adopted as state bird in 1933.

State Rock

The geode, a hollow stone with crystals at the center, was named state rock in 1967.

State Songs

"The Song of Iowa," with words set to "Der Tannenbaum" by S. H. M. Byers, was adopted as the state song in 1911. An unofficial state song is the "Iowa Corn Song" by George Hamilton.

Population

The population of Iowa in 1990 was 2,787,424 making it the 30th most populous state. There are 49.5 persons per square mile—58.6 percent of

The wild rose was named state flower in 1897.

the population live in towns and cities. About 80 percent of all Iowans were born in the state, and about 98 percent were born in the United States. About one-fourth of the foreign-born came from Germany.

Geography and Climate

Bounded on the north by Minnesota, on the east by Wisconsin and Illinois, on the south by Missouri, and on the west by Nebraska and South Dakota, Iowa has an area of 56,275 square miles, making it the 25th largest state. The climate is continental and rather humid.

The state is level from northwest to southeast. The highest point in the state, at 1,670 feet, is near Ocheyedan in Osceola County, and the lowest, at 480 feet, is along the Mississippi River in Lee County. The major waterways of the state are the Mississippi, Missouri, Des Moines, Cedar, Iowa, and Wapsipinicon rivers.

Industries

The principal industries in Iowa are wholesale and retail trade, insurance, finance and real estate, and agriculture. The chief manufactured products are tires, farm machinery, electronic products, appliances, office furniture, chemicals, fertilizers, and auto accessories.

Agriculture

The chief crops of the state are silage, grain corn, soybeans, oats, and hay. Iowa is also a livestock state, and there are estimated to be some 4.8 million cattle, 13.5 million hogs and pigs, 400,000 sheep, and 7.6 million turkeys on its farms. Red cedar trees are harvested. Crushed stone, cement, sand, and gravel are important mineral products.

Government

The governor of Iowa is elected to a four-year term, as are the other high executives of the state. The state legislature, called the general assembly, which meets annually, consists of a senate of 50 members and a house of representatives of 100 members, elected from 50 senatorial districts and 100 representative districts. The most recent state constitution was adopted in 1857. In addition to its two U.S. senators, Iowa has five representatives in the U.S. House of Representatives. The state has seven votes in the electoral college.

History

Before the Europeans arrived, the Iowa region was the home of prehistoric Indians called Mound Builders, and later by both Woodland and Plains Indians. Along the Mississippi River lived the Illinois, Iowa, Miami, Ottawa, and Sioux Indian tribes. In the western section were the Omaha, Oto, and Missouri tribes. In the 1700s, these were joined by Sauk and Fox Indians from Wisconsin.

Iowa farmland is among the most fertile and productive in the country.

Father Jacques Marquette and Louis Jolliet were probably the first Europeans to visit the Iowa region when they came down the Wisconsin River in 1673. Robert Cavelier, Sieur de La Salle, claimed the entire Mississippi Valley for France in 1682, naming it Louisiana in honor of King Louis XIV of France. Few people visited the Iowa territory, and no permanent settlements were made for many years.

France ceded the territory west of the Mississippi to Spain in 1762, and in 1788, Julien Dubuque, a French-Canadian adventurer, became the first permanent settler. In 1800, Spain gave

Fort Atkinson was built in 1840 by the Winnebago Indians. It is now the site of a pioneer museum.

part of Louisiana, including the Iowa region, back to France. Iowa became part of the United States in 1803 following the Louisiana Purchase. In 1805, Iowa was included in the Territory of Louisiana, which was explored by Meriwether Lewis and William Clark (1804-06) and Zebulon Pike (1805 and 1806). Finally, in 1808, the first fort in Iowa, Fort Madison, was built.

Iowa became part of the Missouri Territory in 1812, and fur companies built posts along the rivers. In 1834, a section of Iowa became part of the Michigan Territory, and the Territory of Iowa was created in 1838. This contained Iowa, most of Minnesota, and two-thirds of North and South Dakota. Present-day Iowa became the 29th state of the Union in 1846.

Settlers came in droves, most of them anti-slavery advocates, and many Iowa men served in the Union Army during the Civil War. The railroads reached the state in 1867, and farms prospered. Steamboat traffic on the Mississippi also became a big industry. Many Iowa men and women served during World War I. During the Great Depression of the 1930s, many farmers—over half—lost their land.

During World War II, the farms of Iowa supplied corn and pork for the war effort, and after the war, Iowa began to turn into a manufacturing state. Today, the Hawkeye State is an agricultural and industrial giant.

Sports

Iowans have always been keenly interested in sports of all kinds. In 1883, the first American golf course opened in Burlington. The state is also unique in its fervid interest in girls' high school basketball, and, along with Oklahoma, is a hotbed for collegiate wrestling. In football, the University of Iowa won the Rose Bowl in 1957 and 1959.

Major Cities

Cedar Rapids (population 110,243). Settled in 1838, this city is located at the rapids of the Cedar River. It is one of the state's industrial leaders. Cereals, corn products, milk processing machinery, packaged meats, farm hardware, stock feeds, and electronic material are manufactured here.

Things to see in Cedar Rapids: Brucemore (1886), Czech Village, Cedar Rapids Museum of Art, Science Station, Five Seasons Center, Indian Creek Nature Center, Palisades-Kepler State Park, and Wapsipinicon State Park.

Davenport (population 103,264). Founded in 1808 along the Mississippi River, Davenport is part of the Quad Cities metropolitan area (which also includes Bettendorf and the Illinois cities of Moline and Rock Island). It is a trading and manufacturing town, and here are produced machinery, agricultural goods, and food products.

Things to see in Davenport: Davenport Museum of Art, Putnam Museum, Fejervary Park Zoo, Vander Veer Park, West Lake Park, and Scott County Park.

Des Moines (population 191,003). Founded in 1843, the capital city is also the industrial, retailing, financial, and insurance capital of the state. It was originally a fort on the Raccoon and Des Moines rivers, and was opened to settlers in 1845.

Things to see in Des Moines: State Capitol (1871), Des Moines Art Center, Science Center of Iowa, Polk County Heritage Gallery, Salisbury House, Terrace Hill (1869),

Heritage Village, Blank Park Zoo, Botanical Center and the Living History Farms.

Places to Visit

The National Park Service maintains two areas in the state of Iowa: Effigy Mounds National Monument and Herbert Hoover National Historic Site. In addition, there are 65 state recreation areas.

Amana Colonies: Museum of Amana History. The exhibits include a nursery school, crafts and trades, and other items in the history of the Amana Colonies, a communal religious group.

Cedar Falls: Ice House Museum. A round icehouse in which cut natural ice was stored and sold displays equipment and memorabilia.

Decorah: Vesterheim, the Norwegian-American Museum. Exhibits explain the story of the Norwegians in the United States.

Dubuque: Woodward Riverboat Museum. Exhibits explain 300 years of Mississippi River history.

The skyline of Des Moines, Iowa's largest city.

Elk Horn: Danish Windmill. This working windmill was built in Denmark in 1848, and shipped to Iowa.

Fort Dodge: Fort Dodge Historical Museum, Stockade and Fort. A replica of the 1862 fort.

Fort Madison: Lee County Courthouse. Built in 1841, this is the oldest courthouse in continuous use in Iowa.

Indianola: National Balloon Museum. A collection of balloon memorabilia from the Balloon Federation of America is housed here.

Iowa City: Old Capitol. The first capitol of Iowa has been restored to its original appearance.

Newton: Trainland, USA. This toy train museum shows the development of American railroads.

Pella: Pella Historical Village Museum. Twenty restored buildings, including Wyatt Earp's boyhood home, can be visited.

Events

There are many events and organizations that schedule activities of various kinds in the state of Iowa. Here are some of them.

Sports: Creston Hot-Air Balloon Days (Creston), Drake Relays (Des Moines), Tri-State Rodeo (Fort Madison), National Balloon Classic (Indianola), Old Capitol Criterium Bicycle Race (Iowa City), Amana VIP Golf Tournament (Iowa City), Iowa Pro Hot Air Balloon Championship (Oskaloosa), Ottumwa Pro Balloon Races (Ottumwa), Balloon Days (Storm Lake).

Arts and Crafts: Art-a-Fest/Heritage-Fest (Charles City), Antique Show (Fort Madison).

Iowa City is the site of the state's "Old Capitol."

Music: Summerfest (Ames), Band Concerts (Cedar Falls), Glenn Miller Festival (Clarinda), Southwest Iowa Band Jamboree (Clarinda), Bix Beiderbecke Jazz Festival (Davenport), Music on the March (Dubuque), Des Moines Metro Opera (Indianola), Octoberfest of Bands (Maquoketa).

Entertainment: Veishea Spring Festival (Ames), Pufferbilly Days (Boone), Burlington Steamboat Days and the American Music Festival (Burlington), Sturgis Falls Days Celebration (Cedar Falls), All-Iowa Fair (Cedar Rapids), Riverboat Days (Clinton), Great Mississippi Valley Fair (Davenport), Nordic Fest (Decorah), Two Rivers Festival (Des Moines), Iowa State Fair (Des Moines), Dubuque Fest (Dubuque), Winter Sports Festival (Estherville), Kalona Fall Festival (Iowa City), North Iowa Fair (Mason City), Midwest Old Settlers and Threshers Reunion (Mount Pleasant), Southern Iowa Fair (Oskaloosa), Tulip Festival (Pella), River-Cade Festival (Sioux City), Flagfest Summer Festival (Spencer), Santa's Village (Storm Lake), Mesquakie Indian Powwow (Tama), National Cattle Congress (Waterloo), Covered Bridge Festival (Winterset).

Theater: Riverview Park (Clinton), Okoboji Summer Theater (Okoboji).

Bob Feller was a Hall of Fame pitcher who compiled a record of 266 wins and 162 losses over 18 years with the Cleveland Indians.

Famous People

Many famous people were born in the state of Iowa. Here are a few:

Fran Allison 1908-1989, La Porte City. Television hostess of *Kukla, Fran and Ollie*

Cap Anson 1852-1922, Marshalltown. Hall of Fame baseball player

Bix Beiderbecke 1903-1931, Davenport. Jazz cornetist

Eugene Burdick 1918-1965, Sheldon. Novelist: *The Ugly American, Fail-Safe*

Johnny Carson b. 1925, Corning. Television host

Marquis Childs b. 1903, Clinton. Pulitzer Prize-winning columnist

Buffalo Bill Cody 1846-1917, Scott County. Army scout and showman

Mamie Eisenhower 1896-1979, Boone. First lady

Bob Feller b. 1918, Van Meter. Hall of Fame baseball pitcher

Frank J. Fletcher 1885-1973, Marshalltown. World War II admiral

Janet Guthrie b. 1938, Iowa City. Auto racer

James Hall 1887-1951, Colfax. Novelist: *Mutiny on the Bounty, Men Against the Sea*

Herbert Hoover 1874-1964, West Branch. Thirty-first President of the United States

MacKinlay Kantor 1904-1977, Webster City. Pulitzer Prize-winning novelist: *Andersonville, Long Remember*

Ann Landers b. 1918, Sioux City. Advice columnist

Cloris Leachman b. 1926, Des Moines. Academy Award-winning actress: *The Last Picture Show, Young Frankenstein*

John L. Lewis 1880-1969, Lucas. Union leader

Elmer H. Maytag 1883-1940, Newton. Appliance manufacturer

Glenn Miller 1904-1944, Clarinda. Band leader and trombonist

Harriet Nelson b. 1914, Des Moines. Television actress: *The Adventures of Ozzie and Harriet*

John S. Phillips 1861-1949, Council Bluffs. Magazine publisher

Harry Reasoner b. 1923, Dakota City. Television news correspondent

Donna Reed 1921-1986,

Denison. Academy Award-winning actress: *From Here to Eternity, It's A Wonderful Life.*

Lillian Russell 1861-1921, Clinton. Vaudeville singer and actress

Jacob Schick 1877-1937, Des Moines. Shaver manufacturer

Billy Sunday 1862-1935, Ames. Evangelist

Abigail Van Buren b. 1918, Sioux City. Advice columnist

John Wayne 1907-79, Winterset. Academy Award-winning actor: *True Grit, The Shootist*

Andy Williams b. 1930, Wall Lake. Pop singer

Meredith Willson 1902-84, Mason City. Tony Award-winning composer: *The Music Man, The Unsinkable Molly Brown*

Grant Wood 1892-1942, Anamosa. Painter

Colleges and Universities

There are many colleges and universities in Iowa. Here are the more prominent, with their locations, dates of founding, and enrollments.

Briar Cliff College, Sioux City, 1930, 1,120

Buena Vista College, Storm Lake, 1891, 1,045

Clarke College, Dubuque, 1843, 854

Coe College, Cedar Rapids, 1851, 1,217

Cornell College, Mount Vernon, 1853, 1,147

Drake University, Des Moines, 1881, 7,778

Graceland College, Lamoni, 1895, 898

Grinnell College, Grinnell, 1846, 1,233

Iowa State University of Science and Technology, Ames, 1858, 25,489

Iowa Wesleyan College, Mount Pleasant, 1842, 803

Loras College, Dubuque, 1839, 2,054

Luther College, Decorah, 1861, 2,299

Marycrest College, Davenport, 1939, 2,357

Morningside College, Sioux City, 1889, 1,240

Mount Mercy College, Cedar Rapids, 1875, 1,591

Northwestern College, Orange City, 1882, 1,064

St. Ambrose College, Davenport, 1882, 2,300

Simpson College, Indianola, 1860, 1,737

University of Dubuque, Dubuque, 1852, 1,126

University of Iowa, Iowa City, 1847, 28,884

University of Northern Iowa, Cedar Falls, 1876, 11,837

Wartburg College, Waverly, 1852, 1,456

Where To Get More Information

The Tourism Bureau of the Department of Economic Development
200 East Grand Avenue
Des Moines, IA 50309
Or Call 1-800-345 IOWA

Minnesota

The state seal of Minnesota was adopted in 1858. It is circular, and on it is a rural scene, with a farmer plowing a field and an Indian riding a horse toward the setting sun. In the distance are a waterfall and a forest. In the foreground is the farmer's rifle and powderhorn leaning against a stump. Above the picture is a banner bearing the state motto. Surrounding the picture is printed "The Great Seal of the State of Minnesota" and "1858"—the date of the state's entry into the Union.

State Flag

The state flag, adopted in 1957, contains a white circle with a yellow border on a field of blue. Inside the circle, scenes from the state seal are reproduced in full color. Underneath is the word "Minnesota", and surrounding the scene are 19 stars, representing Minnesota's place as the 19th state to be admitted after the original 13.

State Motto

L'Etoile du Nord

The French motto means "Star of the North," and was approved in 1861.

The beauty and solitude of Tuscarora Lake.

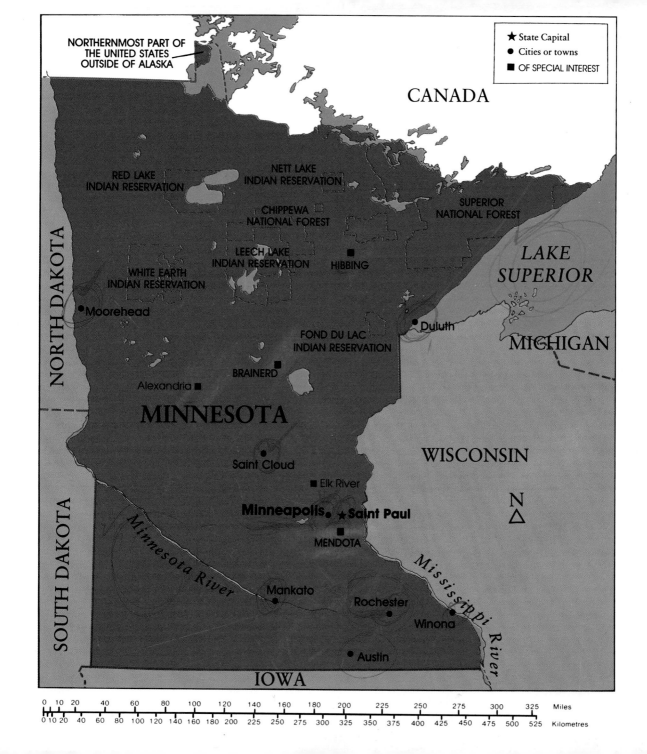

NORTHERNMOST PART OF
THE UNITED STATES
OUTSIDE OF ALASKA

★ State Capital
● Cities or towns
■ OF SPECIAL INTEREST

CANADA

RED LAKE
INDIAN RESERVATION

NETT LAKE
INDIAN RESERVATION

CHIPPEWA
NATIONAL FOREST

SUPERIOR
NATIONAL FOREST

LEECH LAKE
INDIAN RESERVATION

HIBBING

LAKE
SUPERIOR

WHITE EARTH
INDIAN RESERVATION

NORTH DAKOTA

●Moorehead

FOND DU LAC
INDIAN RESERVATION

●Duluth

MICHIGAN

BRAINERD ■

Alexandria ■

MINNESOTA

WISCONSIN

Saint Cloud

■ Elk River

N
△

Minneapolis ● ★Saint Paul

SOUTH DAKOTA

■
MENDOTA

Minnesota River

Mankato ●

Rochester ●

Mississippi River

Winona ●

● Austin

IOWA

| 0 | 10 | 20 | | 40 | | 60 | | 80 | | 100 | | 120 | | 140 | | 160 | | 180 | | 200 | | 225 | | 250 | | 275 | | 300 | | 325 | Miles |

0 10 20   40   60   80   100 120 140 160 180 200 225 250 275 300 325 350 375 400 425 450 475 500 525   Kilometres

The capitol building in St. Paul.

State Capital

St. Paul was named the capital city in 1849, and Minnesota has had no other capital. The present capitol building was opened in 1905, and cost $4.5 million. It is a classic Renaissance structure with a dome, and is located on a hill overlooking the city.

State Name and Nicknames

In the language of the Dakota Indians, the name of the Minnesota River was *Mnishota*, which means "cloudy (or milky) water." The state took its name from the river.

Because of its motto, Minnesota is often called the *North Star State*. Other nicknames are the *Land of 10,000 Lakes* (although it has far more than that), the *Gopher State* (for the many gophers that used to be found on the prairies), and the *Bread and Butter State*

The pink-and-white lady slipper is the state flower.

(because of its production of wheat and dairy products).

State Flower

The pink-and-white lady slipper, *Cypripedium reginae*, was named the state flower of Minnesota in 1902.

State Tree

The Norway pine, *Pinus resinosa*, was adopted as state tree in 1953.

State Bird

In 1961, the common loon, *Gavia immer*, was selected as state bird.

State Drink

Because of the importance of the dairy industry, milk was selected as state drink in 1984.

State Fish

The walleye, *Stizostedion vitreum*, was named the state fish in 1965.

State Gem

The Lake Superior agate has been the state gem since 1969.

The common loon is the state bird.

State Grain

Selected in 1977, wild rice, *Zizania aquatica*, is the state grain.

State Mushroom

The morel, *Morchella esculenta*, is the state mushroom, and was adopted in 1984.

State Song

Named in 1945, the state song of Minnesota is "Hail! Minnesota," with music by Truman E. Rickard and words by Truman E. Rickard and Arthur E. Upson.

Population

The population of Minnesota in 1990 was 4,387,029, making it the 20th most populous state. There are 52.0 persons per square mile—66.9 percent of the population live in towns and cities. About 96 percent of the people in the state were born in the United States. Of the foreign-born, most came from Denmark, Finland, Norway, and Sweden.

Geography and Climate

Bounded on the north by the Canadian provinces of Manitoba and Ontario, on the east by Lake Superior and Wisconsin, on the south by Iowa, and on the west by North and South Dakota, Minnesota has an area of 84,402 square miles, making it the 12th largest state. The climate is variable, with cold winters and hot summers. The northern part of the state is moist, and the southern part is semi-arid.

Approximately half of the state is a region of hills and lakes. To the northeast are rocky ridges and many deep lakes, to the northwest is a flat plain, and to the south are rolling plains and deep river valleys. The highest point in the state, at 2,301 feet, is Eagle Mountain in Cook County. The lowest point, at 600 feet, is along Lake Superior. The major waterways in Minnesota are the Mississippi, Crow Wing, Minnesota, Rum, St. Croix, Sauk, Rainy, Red, and St. Louis rivers. The largest lake completely within the borders of the state is Red Lake.

Industries

The principal industries of the state of Minnesota are farming, forest products, mining, and tourism. The chief manufactured products are processed foods, non-electrical machinery, chemicals, paper, electric and electronic equipment, printing and publishing, instruments, and fabricated metal products.

Agriculture

The chief crops of the state are corn, soybeans, wheat, sugar beets, sunflowers, and barley. Minnesota is also a livestock state, and there are estimated to be some 2.9 million cattle, 4.7 million hogs and pigs, 263,000 sheep, and 11.7 million chickens and turkeys on its farms. Needled and hardwood trees are harvested. Iron ore, sand,

The scenic cliffs of North Shore at Palisade Head.

gravel, and crushed stone are important mineral resources. Commercial fishing brings in some $73,000 per year.

Government

The governor of Minnesota is elected to a four-year term, as are the lieutenant governor, secretary of state, attorney general, treasurer, and auditor. The state legislature, which meets for a total of 120 days within every two years, consists of a 67-member senate and a 134-member house of representatives. The senators serve four-year terms, and are elected from 67 legislative districts. The representatives serve two-year terms, and from one to three are elected from the 67 legislative districts, depending on population. The most recent state constitution was adopted in 1858. In addition to its two U.S. senators, Minnesota has eight representatives in the U.S. House of Representatives. The state has ten votes in the electoral college.

History

Before the Europeans arrived, what was to become Minnesota was mostly populated by Sioux Indians. Later the Chippewa came in from the east and forced the Sioux from the forests. Probably the first Europeans to enter the area were two French fur traders—Pierre Esprit Radisson and Médart Chouart, Sieur de Groseilliers. They arrived in the territory north of Lake Superior between 1659 and 1661.

About 1679, another Frenchman, Daniel Greysolon, Sieur Dulhut, came to the territory. It was he who claimed the land for King Louis XIV of France. A Belgian missionary, Father Louis Hennepin, followed in 1680. Captured by the Sioux, he became the first European to see the site of present-day Minneapolis. He was rescued by Dulhut.

In 1763, after the French and Indian War, France turned over almost all of its territory east of the Mississippi River to England, and British fur trading companies established posts in eastern Minnesota. After the Revolutionary War, the territory that would be eastern Minnesota belonged to the United States. When the United States acquired the Louisiana Purchase in 1803, the rest of Minnesota became part of the country.

In 1820, American troops built Fort St. Anthony (later to be Fort Snelling), and the area of what was to become Minneapolis-St. Paul became a center of industry. Later a land boom occurred in the St. Croix Valley. Over the years, parts of Minnesota had been included in the territories of Illinois, Indiana, Iowa, Michigan, Missouri, and Wisconsin. The Minnesota Territory was created in 1849, and in 1858, it became the 32nd state in the Union.

In 1861, the Civil War began and Minnesota became the first state to offer troops to the Union Army. But in 1862,

The Mayo Clinic in Rochester is one of the top medical facilities in the country.

the Sioux went on the warpath—at a time when many Minnesota men were away in the war. Hundreds of settlers were killed, and much property was lost. The Sioux were finally defeated by federal troops and Minnesota militiamen.

After the war, industry boomed, and railroads expanded. Flour milling became a big business. The Mayo Clinic (founded in Rochester in 1889) became one of the outstanding medical installations in the world.

During World War I, Minnesota furnished wheat and other grains, plus iron ore, to the war effort and sent thousands of men and women to the armed forces. The state was hit hard by the Great Depression of the 1930s. Farmers lost their property, and some 70 percent of the workers in the iron range were laid off.

Recovery came during World War II, when iron, grain, and lumber were once again in great demand. Again, countless Minnesotans served in uniform. After the war, the state continued to bloom, and today it is an industrial, agricultural, and cultural leader.

Sports

Minnesota is a sports state, and many of its residents are skiing enthusiasts. On the collegiate level, the University of Minnesota has won the NCAA national hockey championship (1974, 1976, 1979), the NCAA national baseball championship (1956, 1960, 1964), and the Rose Bowl football game (1962).

On the professional level, the Minnesota Twins of the American League play baseball in the Hubert H. Humphrey Metrodome in Minneapolis. They share this facility with the Minnesota Vikings of the National Football League. The Minnesota Timberwolves of the National Basketball Association play their games in Target Center in Minneapolis, while the Minnesota North Stars of the National Hockey League play in the Metropolitan Sports Center in Bloomington.

Major Cities

Duluth (population 92,811). Founded in 1856, Duluth is a world port located at the western tip of Lake Superior. It is one of the greatest grain-exporting cities in the country, and it also ships iron ore, coal, limestone, crude oil, and many other products. Duluth is a business, industrial, cultural, recreational, and vacation center.

Things to see in Duluth:
Aerial Lift Bridge, Corps of Engineers Canal Park Marine Museum, Fitger's on the Lake, Leif Erickson Park,

The skyscrapers of Minneapolis, the largest city in the state. The city sits next to the capital St. Paul.

Duluth Zoological Gardens, Skyline Parkway Drive, Enger Tower, Glensheen (1905-08), St. Louis County Heritage and Arts Center, Depot Square, A. M. Chisholm Museum, St. Louis County Historical Society, Lake Superior Museum of Transportation, Tweed Museum of Art, and Marshall W. Alworth Planetarium.

Minneapolis (population 370,951). Settled in 1847, Minnesota's largest city is located on the Mississippi River. Even with its skyscrapers, parks, and industry, it still has a frontier vigor. Its name comes from the Sioux word minne, meaning "water," and the Greek *polis*, meaning "city."

Things to see in Minneapolis:
Nicollet Mall, IDS Tower, St. Anthony Falls, Minnehaha Park, Minneapolis Institute of Arts, Walker Art Center, Bell Museum of Natural History, American Swedish Institute, Minneapolis Grain Exchange, Minneapolis City Hall (1891), Minneapolis Planetarium, Hennepin County Historical Society Museum, Minnesota Transportation Museum,

Lyndale Park, Eloise Butler Wildflower Garden and Bird Sanctuary, and Minnesota Zoo.

St. Paul (population 270,230). Settled in 1840, the capital of Minnesota began as a settlement known as Pig's Eye. There are 90 parks and 30 lakes within a 30-minute drive from the city. It is located across the Mississippi River from Minneapolis.

Things to see in St. Paul:
State Capitol (1896-1905), Minnesota Historical Society, City Hall and Courthouse (1932), Landmark Center, Northwest Center Skyway, Science Museum of Minnesota, Minnesota Museum of Art, Children's Museum, James J. Hill Mansion (1891), Alexander Ramsey House (1872), Gibbs Farm Museum (1854), Town Square Park, Como Park, Indian Mounds Park, and Historic Fort Snelling.

Places to Visit

The National Park Service maintains seven areas in the state of Minnesota: Pipestone National Monument, Grand Portage National Monument,

Voyageurs National Park, St. Croix National Scenic Riverway, Lower St. Croix National Riverway, Chippewa National Forest, and Superior National Forest. In addition, there are 70 state recreation areas.

Alexandria: Kensington Runestone Museum. A sandstone boulder with runic inscriptions dated 1362 (said to be Viking) is the most important exhibit.

Bemidji: Paul Bunyan and Blue Ox. Giant replicas of Bunyan and "Babe," his pet, are on display.

Brainerd: Lumbertown, USA. A replica of an old-time lumber town, it contains a store, school, saloon, and more.

Elk River: Oliver H. Kelley Farm and Interpretive Center. This living-history farm was the birthplace of the National Grange.

Eveleth: U.S. Hockey Hall of Fame. The museum honors American players and the sport.

Grand Portage: Grand Portage National Monument. This is a partially restored fur-trading post.

Hibbing: Hull-Rust Mahoning Mine. One of the largest open-pit iron mines, it

Indians perform a ceremony with a peace pipe in the annual Grand Portage Pow Wow.

stretches for three miles and is known as the "Grand Canyon of Minnesota."

International Falls: Smokey the Bear Statue. This is a giant symbol for the campaign against forest fires.

Little Falls: Charles A. Lindbergh House and Interpretive Center. This was the boyhood home of the aviator.

Mankato: Blue Earth County Historical Society. Indian and pioneer exhibits are housed in an 1871 Victorian mansion.

Moorhead: Heritage-Hjemkomst Interpretive Center. A Viking ship replica is one of the major exhibits.

Sauk Centre: Sinclair Lewis Boyhood Home. The restored home of the Nobel Prize-winning novelist.

Shakopee: Valleyfair. This is a turn-of-the-century theme amusement park.

Tracy: Laura Ingalls Wilder Museum and Tourist Center. The museum, a tribute to the novelist, is in an old railroad depot.

Two Harbors: Lake County Historical and Railroad

Museum. The museum in a depot features old locomotives, including a 1941 Mallet.

Events

There are many events and organizations that schedule activities of various kinds in the state of Minnesota. Here are some of them.

Sports: Operation Jumpfest (Albert Lea), Arabian Horse Show (Albert Lea), Brainerd International Raceway (Brainerd), John Beargrease Sled Dog Marathon (Duluth), All-American Championship Sled Dog Races (Ely), "Wilderness Trek" (Ely), Scout Fishing Derby (Glenwood), Last Chance Curling Bonspiel (Hibbing), Jackson National Sprint Car Races (Jackson), International Rolle Bolle Tournament (Marshall), Aquatennial Festival (Minneapolis), Vasaloppet-Cross-Country Ski Race (Mora), Muskie Northern Derby Days (Walker).

Arts and Crafts: Blueberry / Art Festival (Ely).

Music: Scandinavian Folkfest (Detroit Lakes), WE Country Music Fest (Detroit Lakes), Lake Superior Old Time Fiddler's Contest (Duluth), International Folk Festival (Duluth), New

Dance Ensemble (Minneapolis), Minnesota Orchestra (Minneapolis), Sommerfest (Minneapolis), The Glockenspiel (New Ulm), The Rochester Carillon (Rochester), Rochester Symphony Orchestra (Rochester), Minnesota Opera Company (St. Paul), St. Paul Chamber Orchestra (St. Paul), Sonshine Festival (Willmar).

Entertainment: Halloween Festival (Anoka), National Barrow Show (Austin), Paul Bunyan Water Carnival (Bemidji), Lumberjack Days (Cloquet), Red River Valley Winter Shows (Crookston), Northwest Water Carnival (Detroit Lakes), Soo Line Days (Glenwood), Fisherman's Picnic (Grand Marais), Judy Garland Festival (Grand Rapids), Tall Timber Days and U.S. Chainsaw Carving Championships (Grand Rapids), Itasca County Fair (Grand Rapids), Rivertown Days (Hastings), Ethnic Days (Hibbing), Ice Box Days (International Falls), Renaissance Festival (Minneapolis), Victorian Christmas (Minneapolis), Prairie Pioneer Days (Morris), Fasching (New Ulm), Heritagefest (New Ulm), Defeat of Jesse James Days (Northfield), Perham Pioneer Festival (Perham), River City Days (Red Wing), Minnesota Inventors Congress (Redwood Falls), Winter Carnival (St. Paul),

Minnesota's cold and snowy climate is conducive to cross-country skiing.

Macalester College Scottish Country Fair (St. Paul), Minnesota State Fair (St. Paul), Winterfest (Sauk Centre), Sinclair Lewis Days (Sauk Centre), Ag Days and Corn Feed (Spring Valley), Lumberjack Days (Stillwater), Box Car Days (Tracy), Eelpout Festival (Walker), Steamboat Days (Winona), Weekend Wildlife Show (Winona), Victorian Fair (Winona), King Turkey Days and Great Gobbler Gallop (Worthington).

Tours: Historic Walking Tour (Hastings), Walking Tour (Minneapolis).

Theater: Paul Bunyan Playhouse (Bemidji), Mississippi Melodie Showboat (Grand Rapids), Guthrie Theater (Minneapolis), Showboat (Minneapolis), University Theatre (Minneapolis), Straw Hat Summer Theater (Moorhead), Northfield Arts Guild Theater (Northfield), Song of Hiawatha Pageant (Pipestone), Rochester Civic Theater (Rochester), Laura Ingalls Wilder Pageant (Tracy).

Famous People

Many famous people were born in the state of Minnesota. Here are a few:

Robert Bly b. 1926, Madison. Poet: *The Light Around the Body, Point Reyes Poems*

Warren E. Burger b. 1907, St. Paul. Supreme Court Chief Justice

William O. Douglas 1898-1980, Maine. Supreme Court justice

Bob Dylan b. 1941, Duluth. Folk singer

Richard G. Eberhart b. 1904, Austin. Pulitzer Prize-winning poet: *Selected Poems, Brotherhood of Men*

Mike Farrell b. 1939, St. Paul. Television actor: *M*A*S*H*

F. Scott Fitzgerald 1896-1940, St. Paul. Novelist: *The Great Gatsby, Tender Is the Night*

Judy Garland 1922-1969, Grand Rapids. Academy Award-winning actress: *The Wizard of Oz, A Star Is Born*

J. Paul Getty 1892-1976,

F. Scott Fitzgerald was a novelist who wrote about people with wealth and privilege in the roaring 20's.

Minneapolis. Oil company executive

Garrison Keillor b. 1942, Anoka. Writer and radio personality: *Lake Wobegon Days, A Prairie Home Companion*

Sinclair Lewis 1884-1951, Sauk Centre. Nobel Prize-wining novelist: *Elmer Gantry, Dodsworth*

John Madden b. 1936, Austin. Professional football coach and television commentator

Roger Maris 1934-85, Hibbing. Baseball player

Charles Horace Mayo 1865-1939, Rochester. Co-founder of the Mayo Clinic

William James Mayo 1861-1939, Le Sueur. Co-founder of the Mayo Clinic

Eugene McCarthy b. 1916, Watkins. Presidential candidate

Kate Millett b. 1934, St. Paul. Feminist

Walter Mondale b. 1928, Ceylon. Presidential candidate

Ernie Nevers 1903-76, Willow River. Hall of Fame football player

Harrison E. Salisbury b. 1908, Minneapolis. Pulitzer Prize-winning newspaper correspondent

Charles Schulz b. 1922, Minneapolis. Creator of *Peanuts*

Richard W. Sears 1863-1914, Stewartville. Merchant

De Witt Wallace 1889-1981, St. Paul. Founder of the *Reader's Digest*

Richard Widmark b. 1914, Sunrise. Film actor: *Kiss of Death, Against All Odds*

Colleges and Universities

There are many colleges and universities in Minnesota. Here are the more prominent, with their locations, dates of founding, and enrollments.

Augsburg College, Minneapolis, 1869, 2,702

Bemidji State University, Bemidji, 1913, 5,150

Bethel College, St. Paul, 1871, 1,832

Carleton College, Northfield, 1866, 1,850

College of Saint Benedict, Saint Joseph, 1913, 1,872

College of St. Catherine, St. Paul, 1906, 2,585

College of St. Scholastica, Duluth, 1912, 1,900

College of St. Thomas, St. Paul, 1885, 9,120

Concordia College, Moorhead, 1891, 2,884

Concordia College, St. Paul, 1893, 1,128

Gustavus Adolphus College, St. Peter, 1862, 2,349

Hamline University, St. Paul, 1854, 2,235

Macalester College, St. Paul, 1853, 1,855

Mankato State University, Mankato, 1866, 16,185

Moorhead State University, Moorhead, 1885, 8,793

St. Cloud State University, St. Cloud, 1866, 16,551

Saint John's University, Collegeville, 1857, 2,003

Saint Mary's College of Minnesota, Winona, 1912, 3,273

St. Olaf College, Northfield, 1874, 3,132

University of Minnesota, Morris, Morris, 1959, 2,041; *Twin Cities Campus,* Minneapolis, 1851, 41,016

Winona State University, Winona, 1858, 7,500

Where To Get More Information

Minnesota Travel Information Center
250 Skyway Level
375 Jackson Street
St. Paul, MN 55101

Wisconsin

The state seal of Wisconsin, adopted in 1851, is nearly identical to the state coat of arms pictured here. In the center is a shield with a plow in the upper left corner, a pick and shovel in the upper right, an anchor in the lower right, and an arm and hand holding a hammer in the lower left. These represent agriculture, mining, navigation, and industry. In the center of the shield is a smaller shield with the coat of arms of the United States, over which is printed *E Pluribus Unum*, Latin for "out of many, one"—the motto of the nation. To the left of the larger shield is a sailor holding a coil of rope, and on the right is a miner resting on his pick. Below the shield is a horn of plenty and a pyramid of pig lead. Above the shield is a badger. Over the badger is a banner with the word "Forward"—the state motto. In addition, the state seal has the words "Great Seal of the State of Wisconsin" at the top, and 13 stars on a banner at the bottom.

State Flag

The state flag contains the state seal on a blue background, with the word Wisconsin above it, and below it the date 1848, the year Wisconsin became a state. It was adopted in 1981.

State Motto

Forward

This motto became official in 1851.

Frank Lloyd Wright designed the House on the Rock.

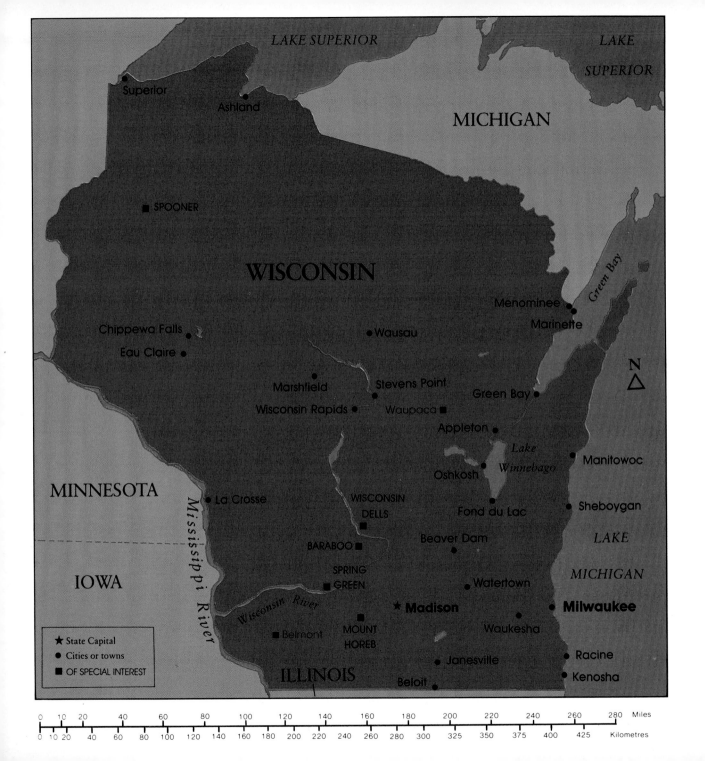

The state capitol building in Madison.

State Capital

Before Wisconsin became a state, the capital of the territory was in Belmont (1836), Burlington (now in Iowa, 1837), and Madison (1838-48). Madison has been the capital ever since. The present capitol building was completed in 1917, and cost $7.5 million. Located in the center of a 13.4-acre park between lakes Mendota and Monona, the Roman Renaissance building is made of marble and granite. A gilded bronze statue, *Wisconsin*, by Daniel Chester French, is located on top of the granite dome.

State Name and Nicknames

In Chippewa, *Wisconsin* meant "grassy place," and that is what the Indians called the Wisconsin River. The state was named after the river.

Although it is unofficial, the most common nickname of Wisconsin is the *Badger State*, named for the early lead miners who lived underground and bore this nickname. Wisconsin is also known as the *Copper State* in honor of its copper mines.

State Flower

The wood violet, *Viola papilionacea*, was adopted as the state flower in 1949. The flower was selected in 1909 by schoolchildren, who had to choose between the violet, the wild rose, the trailing arbutus, and the white water lily.

State Tree

Wisconsin schoolchildren voted in 1948 and selected the sugar maple, *Acer saccharum*, as the state tree.

The wood violet is the state flower.

That choice was made official in 1949.

State Bird

Wisconsin schoolchildren voted for the robin, *Turdus migratorius*, in 1926-27, but the state legislature did not make it official state bird until 1949.

State Animal

The badger, *Taxidea taxus*, was selected state animal in 1957.

State Domestic Animal

The dairy cow has been the state domestic animal since 1971.

State Fish

The muskellunge, *Esox masquinongy*, was named state fish in 1955.

State Insect

The honeybee, *Apis mellifera*, was adopted as state insect in 1977.

State Mineral

Galena, the chief ore of lead, was selected in 1971.

State Rock

Red granite was adopted as state rock in 1971.

State Soil

Antigo silt loam has been the state soil since 1983.

The robin is the state bird.

State Symbol of Peace

The mourning dove, *Zenaidura macroura*, was named in 1971.

State Wildlife Animal

In 1957, the white-tailed deer, *Odocoileus virginianus,* was adopted as the state wildlife animal.

State Song

Originally written as a football fight song in 1909, "On, Wisconsin!" with words by J.S. Hubbard and Charles D. Rosa and music by William T. Purdy, was named the state song in 1959, although the lyrics had to be changed.

Population

The population of Wisconsin in 1990 was 4,906,745, making it the 16th most populous state. There are 87.4 persons per square mile—64.2 percent of the population live in towns and cities. About 97 percent of the people in Wisconsin were born in the United States.

Indians scale the rocks of Wisconsin Dells, one of the state's most scenic regions.

Most of the foreign-born came from Canada, Germany, Italy, Poland, Russia, and Yugoslavia.

Geography and Climate

Bounded on the north by Lake Superior and Michigan, on the east by Michigan and Lake Michigan, on the south by Illinois, and on the west by Iowa and Minnesota,

Wisconsin has an area of 56,153 square miles, making it the 26th largest state. Although the climate is tempered by the Great Lakes, the winters are long and cold and the summers are short and hot.

Near Lake Superior is a lowland plain, and south of that are highlands. There is a plain in the middle of the state, uplands in the southwest and lowlands in the southeast. The highest point in the state, at 1,951 feet, is Timms Hill in Price County. The lowest point, at 579 feet, is along Lake Michigan. The major waterways of the state are the Bad, Montreal, Nemadji, Flambeau, St. Croix, Black, Chippewa, Wisconsin, Fox, Menominee, Milwaukee, Mississippi, Oconto, and Peshtigo rivers. The largest lake inside the borders of Wisconsin is Lake Winnebago.

Industries

The principal industries of Wisconsin are trade, services, transportation, communications, and agriculture. The chief manufactured products are machinery, foods, fabricated metals, transportation equipment, and paper and wood products.

Agriculture

The chief crops of the state are corn, beans, beets, peas, hay, oats, cabbage, and cranberries, and the chief products are milk, butter, and cheese. Wisconsin is also a livestock state, and there are estimated to be some 4.1 million cattle, 1.3 million hogs and pigs, 84,000 sheep, and 4.1 million chickens and turkeys on its farms. Maple, birch, oak, and evergreen trees are harvested. Crushed stone, sand, gravel, and lime are important mineral products. Commercial fishing brings in some $5.6 million per year.

Government

The governor of Wisconsin is elected for a four-year term, as are the lieutenant

Wisconsin's vast stretches of farmland are beautiful examples of one of the state's major industries, agriculture.

governor, secretary of state, attorney general, treasurer, and state superintendent of public instruction. The legislature consists of a 33-member senate and a 99-member assembly. Senators are elected from 33 senatorial districts and serve four-year terms. Assemblymen are elected from 99 assembly districts and serve two-year terms. The most recent state constitution was adopted in

1848. In addition to its two U.S. senators, Wisconsin has nine representatives in the U.S. House of Representatives. The state has 11 votes in the electoral college.

History

Before the Europeans arrived in what was to become Wisconsin, it was populated by the Winnebago (between Green Bay and Lake Winnebago), the Dakota (in the northwest), and the Menominee (west and north of Green Bay). Later, in the 1600s, other Indians moved into the territory—the Chippewa, Sauk, Fox, Ottawa, Kickapoo, Huron, Miami, Illinois, and Potawatomi.

The first European to visit the area was a Frenchman, Jean Nicolet, who landed on the shore of present-day Green Bay in 1634. About 25 years later, Pierre Esprit Radisson and Médart Chouart, Sieur de Groseilliers, explored the territory while looking for furs. About 1660, Father René Ménard founded a mission near present-day Ashland, and two other priests established a missionary center on the site of today's De Pere.

After the French and Indian War, France turned control of the Wisconsin region over to the British. English fur traders explored the territory, but after the Revolutionary War, Wisconsin became part of the United States. Wisconsin was a segment of the Indiana Territory (1800-09), part of the Illinois Territory (1809-18), and part of the Michigan Territory (1818-36) before becoming the Wisconsin Territory in 1836. In 1848, Wisconsin became the 30th state of the Union. During the Civil War, one of the most valiant of all the Union Army units was the Iron Brigade, consisting mainly of Wisconsin regiments.

Wisconsin men and women served bravely in both World War I and World War II. Today, the state is a leader in agriculture, industry, and education.

Sports

Wisconsin is a sports state. On the collegiate level, the University of Wisconsin has won the NCAA national hockey championship (1973,

The Landfall of Nicolet at Red Banks, 1679 *is a painting depicting the landing of European explorers on the shores of Wisconsin.*

1977, 1981, 1983, 1990) and the NCAA national basketball championship (1941). Marquette University has won the NCAA national basketball championship (1977) and the National Invitation Tournament (1970).

On the professional level, the Milwaukee Brewers of the American League play baseball in Milwaukee County Stadium, and the Green Bay Packers of the National Football League play at Lambeau Field and County Stadium. The Milwaukee Bucks of the National Basketball Association play their games at the Bradley Center.

Major Cities

Green Bay (population 87,899). Settled in 1764, Green Bay is Wisconsin's second-busiest port. The region was claimed for King Louis XII of France in 1634, and was named La Baye in 1669 when it became the site of a mission. It is the oldest settlement in the state.

Things to see in Green Bay: Heritage Hill State Park, Beaupre Place (1840), Baird Law Office (1835), Roi-Porlier-Tank Cottage (1750), Fort Howard (1833-34), Neville Public Museum, National Railroad Museum, Hazelwood (1837-38), Green Bay Packer Hall of Fame, and Bay Beach Amusement Park and Wildlife Sanctuary.

Madison (population 170,616). Settled in 1837, Madison was a wilderness when the site was selected to be the capital of the territory in 1836. This "City of Four Lakes" is today a center of government and education. It has a rich architectural heritage left by Frank Lloyd Wright and the Prairie School movement.

Things to see in Madison: State Capitol, G. A. R. Memorial Hall Museum, State Historical Museum, Elvehjem Museum of Art, Madison Art Center, Henry Vilas Park Zoo, Olbrich Gardens, First Unitarian Church, Bradley House, Airplane House, Dr. Arnold Jackson House, Lamp House, J. C. Pew House, "Jacobs I" House, U.S.D.A. Forest

Products Laboratory, and Dane County Farmers' Market.

Milwaukee (population 636,236). Settled in 1822, Wisconsin's largest city was incorporated as a city in 1846. It was called *Millioki* by the Indians, which meant "gathering place by the waters." Today, "the machine shop of America" is one of the nation's top industrial cities.

Things to see in Milwaukee: War Memorial Center, Milwaukee Art Museum, Villa Terrace, Charles Allis Art Museum, Bradford Beach, City Hall (1895), Pabst Theater (1895), Milwaukee County Historical Center, Old World Third Street, Milwaukee Public Museum, Court of Honor, Northwestern Coffee Mills, St. Joan of Arc Chapel, Haggerty Museum of Art, Captain Frederick Pabst Mansion (1893), Milwaukee County Zoo, Mitchell Park Horticultural Conservatory, Annunciation Greek Orthodox Church, Lowell Damon House (1844), Kilbourntown House (1844), Schlitz Audubon Center, and Whitnall Park.

The exhibits at the Milwaukee Public Museum reflect the natural and human history of the state.

Places to Visit

The National Park Service maintains five areas in the state of Wisconsin: Apostle Islands National Lakeshore, Ice Age National Scientific Reserve, St. Croix National Scenic Riverway, Chequamegon National Forest, and Nicolet National Forest. In addition, there are 54 state recreation areas.

Baileys Harbor: Bjorklunden. A replica of a Norwegian chapel, or *stavkirke*, is located on this 325-acre estate.

Baraboo: Circus World Museum. This museum displays equipment used by the Ringling brothers' circus, which started here in 1884.

Belmont: First Capitol State Park. The 1836 council house and supreme court building have been restored.

Downsville: Caddie Woodlawn Country Park. Two 100-year-old houses and a log smokehouse are located in this memorial to the pioneer girl made famous in *Caddie Woodlawn* and *Magical Melons*.

Eagle: Old World Wisconsin. An outdoor museum recreates the pioneer life of German, Norwegian, Danish, and Finnish farmers.

Eagle River: Trees for Tomorrow Natural Resources Education Center. Demonstration forests and nature trails are part of this environmental education development.

Eau Claire: Paul Bunyan Logging Camp. This is a restored 40-man logging camp, with several 19th-century buildings.

Egg Harbor: Chief Oshkosh Indian Museum. This museum contains the possessions of the Menominee Indian chief and other Indian artifacts.

Ephraim: Pioneer Schoolhouse Museum. A restored schoolhouse (1869) and log cabin (1857) are among the exhibits.

Manitowoc: Maritime Museum. The World War II submarine USS *Cobia* can be toured.

Mineral Point: Pendarvis, Cornish Restoration. Six restored log and limestone homes built by English miners in the 1840s are located here.

Minocqua: Jim Peck's Wildwood. This 30-acre park houses hundreds of animals native to the area.

Mount Horeb: Little Norway. A small Norwegian farmstead, including a wooden church, or *stavkirke*, dates back to 1856.

New Glarus: Swiss Historical Village. Replicas of the first buildings erected by settlers in the 1840s can be seen here.

Port Washington: Lizard Mound. Thirty-one examples of effigy mounds built by prehistoric Wisconsin Indians.

Prairie du Chien: Fort Crawford Medical Museum. Relics of 19th-century medicine are on display.

Rhinelander: Rhinelander Logging Museum. Exhibits describing the logging history of the area.

Richland Center: Eagle Cave. This large onyx cavern has stalactites, stalagmites, and fossils.

Spring Green: Taliesin Fellowship Buildings. This was the 200-acre estate of the architect Frank Lloyd Wright.

Washington Island: Rock Island State Park. Icelandic-style architecture and the Potawatomi Lighthouse (1836) can be seen here.

Watertown: Octagon House and First Kindergarten in the U.S.A. The house, built in 1854, contains a hanging staircase. The kindergarten, which began in 1856, was housed separately.

Waupaca: Doll Shop Museum. More than 3,500 antique and modern dolls and a large teddy bear display may be seen here.

Wisconsin Dells: Wisconsin Dells State Recreation Area. The Wisconsin River cut a seven-mile channel through soft sandstone, forming tall cliffs and strange rock formations, which can be seen on guided tours by boat.

Events

There are many events and organizations that schedule activities of various kinds in the state of Wisconsin. Here are some of them.

Sports: Bay Days Festival (Ashland), Sno-Escapades (Bayfield), Musky Jamboree (Boulder Junction), American Birkebeiner (Cable), World Championship Snowmobile Derby (Eagle River), Chicago Historic Races' International Challenge (Elkhart Lake), Road America (Elkhart Lake), Walleye Weekend Festival and National Walleye Tournament (Fond du Lac), International Aerobatic

Deer and other wildlife roam Jim Peck's Wildwood, a 30-acre park in Minocqua.

Championship (Fond du Lac), Lumberjack World Championships (Hayward), Paddle and Portage Canoe Race (Madison), World Championship Musky Classic (Manitowish Waters), Salmon-A-Rama (Racine), Great Wisconsin Dells Balloon Rally (Wisconsin Dells).

Arts and Crafts: Cherry and Apple Blossom Time (Baileys Harbor), Art Fair on the Square (Madison), E. K. Petrie's Indian Artifact and Antique Show and Sale (Oshkosh), Outdoor Arts Festival (Sheboygan).

Music: Wisconsin Opry (Baraboo), Dixieland Jazz Festival (Eau Claire), Birch Creek Music Center (Egg Harbor), Madison Symphony (Madison), Concerts on the Square (Madison), Marquette Hall's 48-Bell Carillon (Milwaukee), Milwaukee Ballet (Milwaukee), Florentine Opera of Milwaukee (Milwaukee), Skylight Opera Theatre (Milwaukee), Milwaukee Symphony (Milwaukee).

Entertainment: Wisconsin State Maple Syrup Festival and Pancake Day (Antigo), Croatian Day (Ashland), Apple Festival (Bayfield), Beaverfest (Beaver Dam), Winnebago Indian Pow-Wow (Black River Falls), Winter Festival (Cedarburg), Northern Wisconsin State Fair (Chippewa

The Milwaukee Summerfest celebrates summer every year with carnival rides, food and games.

Falls), Old Ellison Bay Days (Ellison Bay), Fyr-Bal Fest (Ephraim), Wisconsin Folk Festival (Fond du Lac), Waterboard Warriors (Green Bay), Indian powwows (Lac du Flambeau), La Crosse Interstate Fair (La Crosse), Venetian Festival (Lake Geneva), Dairyfest (Marshfield), Swiss Volksfest (New Glarus), Wilhelm Tell Festival (New Glarus), Old Copper Festival (Oconto), Waterfest (Oshkosh), EAA International Fly-In Convention (Oshkosh), Butter Festival (Reedsburg), Aquafest (Rice

Lake), Richland Centerfest (Richland Center), Wannigan Days (St. Croix Falls), Holland Festival (Sheboygan), Sister Bay Fall Festival (Sister Bay), Head-of-the-Lakes Fair (Superior), Cranberry Festival (Tomah), Scandinavian Festival (Washington Island), Wisconsin Valley Fair (Wausau), Stand Rock Indian Ceremonial (Wisconsin Dells).

Tours: Stone and Century House Tour (Cedarburg), Fall Flyway Tours (Fond du Lac), House and Garden Walk (Sturgeon Bay).

Theater: Cloak Theater (Appleton), Alpine Valley Music Theater (Elkhorn), Peninsula Players (Fish Creek), Theatre on the Bay (Marinette), Mabel Tainter Chautauqua of the Pinery (Menominee), Pabst Theater (Milwaukee), Performing Arts Center (Milwaukee), Northern Lights Summer Playhouse (Minocqua), *Song of Norway* (Mount Horeb), Wisconsin Shakespeare Festival (Platteville), American Players Theatre (Spring Green).

Famous People

Many famous people were born in the state of Wisconsin. Here are a few:

John Bardeen 1908-1991, Madison. Two-time Nobel Prize-winning physicist

Carrie Chapman Catt 1859-1947, Ripon. Women's rights leader

Herbert S. Gasser 1888-1963, Platteville. Noble Prize-winning physiologist

Arnold L. Gesell 1880-1961, Alma. Child psychologist

King C. Gillette 1855-1932, Fond du Lac. Safety razor manufacturer

The magician and escape artist Harry Houdini spent his life getting out of ropes, shackles, and various locked containers.

Eric Heiden b. 1958, Madison. Olympic gold medal-winning speed skater

Harry Houdini 1874-1926, Appleton. Magician

Curly Lambeau 1898-1965, Green Bay. Hall of Fame football coach

Liberace 1919-1987, West Allis. Pianist

Alfred Lunt 1893-1977, Milwaukee. Stage actor

Fredric March 1897-1975, Racine. Academy Award-winning actor: *Dr. Jekyll and Mr. Hyde*

Georgia O'Keeffe 1887-1986, Sun Prairie. Painter

William Rehnquist b. 1924, Milwaukee. Supreme Court Chief Justice

John Ringling 1866-1936, near Baraboo. Circus owner

Al Simmons 1902-1956, Milwaukee. Hall of Fame baseball player

Red Smith 1905-1982, Green Bay. Sports writer

Spencer Tracy 1900-1967, Milwaukee. Academy Award-winning actor: *Boys Town, Guess Who's Coming to Dinner*

Orson Welles 1915-1985, Kenosha. Academy Award-winning actor and director: *Citizen Kane*

Gene Wilder b. 1935, Milwaukee. Film actor: *The Producers, Young Frankenstein*

Laura Ingalls Wilder 1867-

1957, Pepin. Novelist: *Little House on the Prairie, On the Banks of Plum Creek*

Thornton Wilder 1897-1975, Madison. Three-time Pulitzer Prize-winning novelist and playwright: *The Bridge of San Luis Rey, Our Town*

Frank Lloyd Wright 1869-1959, Richland Center. Architect

Colleges and Universities

There are many colleges and universities in Wisconsin. Here are the more prominent, with their locations, dates of founding, and enrollments.

Alverno College, Milwaukee, 1887, 2,310

Beloit College, Beloit, 1846, 1,066

Cardinal Stritch College, Milwaukee, 1932, 3,376

Carroll College, Waukesha, 1840, 1,478

Carthage College, Kenosha, 1847, 2,002

Edgewood College, Madison, 1927, 1,252

Lakeland College, Sheboygan, 1862, 1,766

Lawrence University, Appleton, 1847, 1,228

Marian College of Fond du Lac, Fond du Lac, 1936, 1,000

Marquette University, Milwaukee, 1857, 12,025

Mount Mary College, Milwaukee, 1913, 1,420

Ripon College, Ripon, 1851, 829

St. Norbert College, De Pere, 1898, 1,950

University of Wisconsin— Eau Claire, 1916, 10,773; *Green Bay,* 1969, 4,776; *La Crosse,* 1909, 8,984; *Madison,* 1848, 41,100; *Milwaukee,* 1908, 24,857; *Oshkosh,* 1871, 10,881; *Kenosha,* 1969, 5,265; *Platteville,* 1866, 5,430; *River Falls,* 1874, 5,243; *Stevens Point,* 1894, 8,538; *Menomonie,* 1893, 7,322; *Superior,* 1896, 2,561; *Whitewater,* 1868, 10,270

Viterbo College, La Crosse, 1931, 1,147

Where To Get More Information
The Wisconsin Division of Tourism
Box 7606
Madison, WI 53707
Or Call 1-800-ESCAPES

Bibliography

General

Aylesworth, Thomas G. and Virginia L. Aylesworth, *Let's Discover the States: Western Great Lakes.* New York: Chelsea House, 1987.

Illinois

Bridges, Roger D., and Rodney O. Davis. *Illinois, Its History and Legacy.* St. Louis: River City Publishers, 1984.

Carpenter, Allan. *Illinois,* rev. ed. Chicago: Childrens Press, 1979.

Lathrop, Ann, and others. *Illinois: Its People and Culture,* Minneapolis: Denison, 1975

Howard, Robert P. *Illinois: A History of the Prairie State.* Grand Rapids: Eerdman's, 1972.

Jensen, Richard J. *Illinois: A Bicentennial History.* New York: Norton, 1978.

Nelson, Ronald E., ed. *Illinois: Land and Life in the Prairie State.* Dubuque: Kendall/Hunt, 1978.

Iowa

Carpenter, Allan. *Iowa,* rev. ed. Chicago: Childrens Press, 1979.

Fradin, Dennis B. *Iowa in Words and Pictures.* Chicago: Childrens Press, 1980.

Posten, Margaret L. *This Is the Place—Iowa,* 3rd ed. Ames: Iowa State University Press, 1971.

Sage, Leland L. *A History of Iowa.* Ames: Iowa State University Press, 1974.

Wall, Joseph F. *Iowa: A Bicentennial History.* New York: Norton, 1978.

Minnesota

Aylesworth, Thomas G., and Virginia L. Aylesworth, *Minnesota.* Greenwich, CT: Bison Books, 1986.

Blegen, Theodore C. *Minnesota: A History of the State,* 2nd ed. Minneapolis: University of Minnesota Press, 1975.

Carpenter, Allan. *Minnesota,* rev. ed. Chicago: Childrens Press, 1978.

Lass, William E. *Minnesota: A Bicentennial History.* New York: Norton, 1977.

Lass, William E. *Minnesota, A History.* New York: Norton, 1983.

Rosenfelt, Willard E. *Minnesota: Its People and Culture.* Minneapolis: Denison, 1973.

Wisconsin

Austin, H. Russell. *The Wisconsin Story: The Building of a Vanguard State,* 3rd. ed. Milwaukee: Milwaukee Journal, 1964.

Carpenter, Allan. *Wisconsin,* rev. ed. Chicago: Childrens Press, 1978.

Dean, Jill W., ed. *Wisconsin,* Middleton: Tamarack Press, 1978.

Isherwood, Justin. *Wisconsin.* Portland: Graphic Arts Center, 1981.

Nesbit, Robert C. *Wisconsin: A History.* Madison: University of Wisconsin Press, 1973.

Paul, Justus F. and B. D., eds. *The Badger State: A Documentary History of Wisconsin.* Grand Rapids: Eerdman's, 1979.

Photo Credits/Acknowledgments

Photos on pages 3 (top), 5-7, 9, 10-11, 13-15, 17, courtesy of Illinois Department of Commerce and Community Affairs; pages 22-23, 25-30, courtesy of Iowa Department of Economic Development; pages 3 (middle) and 21 courtesy of Iowa Governor's Office and the Iowa State Printing Office; pages 34-35, 38-39, 41-44, courtesy of Minnesota Office of Tourism; pages 3 (bottom) and 33 courtesy of Minnesota Secretary of State; pages 48-49, 51-54, 57-59, courtesy of Wisconsin Division of Tourism; pages 4 and 47 courtesy of Wisconsin Secretary of State; page 14 courtesy of Terry Farmer; page 31 courtesy of UPI; page 45 courtesy of Macmillan Publishing Company; pages 55 and 60 courtesy of the State Historical Society of Wisconsin.

Cover photograph courtesy of Wisconsin Division of Tourism.